YOUNG ARCHITECT

Ancient Homes

by Saranne Taylor

Illustrated by Moreno Chiacchiera and Michelle Todd

Crabtree Publishing Company

Crabtree Publishing Company
www.crabtreebooks.com
1-800-387-7650

Published in Canada
616 Welland Ave.
St. Catharines, ON
L2M 5V6

Published in the United States
PMB 59051, 350 Fifth Ave.
59th Floor,
New York, NY

Author: Saranne Taylor
Illustrators: Moreno Chiacchiera, Michelle Todd
Project coordinator: Kelly McNiven
Editor: Shirley Duke
Proofreader: Crystal Sikkens
**Production coordinator and
 prepress technician:** Ken Wright
Print coordinator: Katherine Berti

Photographs:
Pg 4 – javarmana
Pg 10 - YURY TARANIK
Pg 11 – (t) jo Crebbin (b) Byelikova Oksana
Pg 12 – vitmark
Pg 16 - (l) Andrey_Kuzman (m) Berents (r) pasphotography
Pg 21 - Rudolf Tepfenhart
Pg 22 – Wikipedia
Pg 23 – (t) LianeM (bl) Alexey Khromushin (br) antb
Pg 26/27 - andrea muscatello
Pg 28 – (t) f8grapher (b) Rigamondis
Pg 29 – (tl) perspectivestock (tr) jocic
Pg 29 – (bl) mountainpix (br) r.nagy

All images are Shutterstock.com unless otherwise stated.

Every attempt has been made to clear copyright. Should there
be any inadvertent omissions, please notify the publisher.

Printed in Hong Kong/082014/BK20140613

Library and Archives Canada Cataloguing in Publication

Taylor, Saranne, author
    Ancient homes / written by Saranne Taylor ; illustrated by Moreno
Chiacchiera and Michelle Todd.

(Young architect)
Includes index.
Issued in print and electronic formats.
ISBN 978-0-7787-1437-8 (bound).--ISBN 978-0-7787-1453-8 (pbk.).--
ISBN 978-1-4271-1576-8 (pdf).--ISBN 978-1-4271-1569-0 (html)

    1. Dwellings--History--Juvenile literature. I. Chiacchiera, Moreno,
illustrator II. Todd, Michelle, 1978-, illustrator III. Title.

TH4808.T39 2014   j728   C2014-903767-8
                                       C2014-903768-6

Library of Congress Cataloging-in-Publication Data

Taylor, Saranne.
 Ancient homes / by Saranne Taylor ; illustrated by Moreno Chiacchiera and Michelle
Todd.
    pages cm. -- (Young architect)
 Includes index.
 ISBN 978-0-7787-1437-8 (reinforced library binding) -- ISBN 978-0-7787-1453-8 (pbk.)
ISBN 978-1-4271-1576-8 (electronic pdf) -- ISBN 978-1-4271-1569-0 (electronic html)
1. Dwellings--Juvenile literature. 2. Architecture, Domestic--Juvenile literature. 3.
Architecture, Ancient--Juvenile literature. I. Chiacchiera, Moreno, illustrator. II. Todd
Michelle, 1978- illustrator. III. Title.

NA7105.T38 2015
722--dc23

                              2014020970

Contents

Introduction

What was it like to live in ancient times? What sort of houses were built then? Thanks to scientists and **archaeologists** we know quite a lot about the amazing architects and engineers who lived back then—even more than 12,000 years ago! They weren't as different from us as you might think.

The city of Shibam, Hadhramaut

Mud towers

Shibam is a stunning city in the Arab country of Yemen. It was built on the **site** where traders used to buy and sell their goods. Some of its buildings were built over a thousand years ago, but most of what we see today was built in the 1500s—still over 500 years ago!

The city is a good example of early housing because all the buildings are made with sun-dried mud bricks or clay. The dried brick is one of the traditional **materials** of older architecture.

Shibam is also interesting because the buildings are like blocks of towers. It is sometimes called the oldest skyscraper city in the world.

A high, **fortified** wall surrounds the well-designed buildings of Shibam. The streets are laid out in a crisscross arrangement. This design shows the excellent **engineering** and planning that took place hundreds of years ago.

Inside an ancient site

The ancient homes are tall towers built close together above a river to avoid the dangerous floodwaters.

A high wall surrounds the city to keep out enemies.

The buildings are narrow. There are often only one or two rooms on each floor.

Windows are high up for protection from enemies.

The layout of the city is on a grid plan which makes it well-organized and orderly.

The buildings are taken care of and repaired by adding new layers of mud every few years.

Scientists called archaeologists study ancient sites like these to learn about the people of the past and the way they lived.

Interesting ruins, which are the remains of even older buildings, are often found near old towns like Shibam.

palace

mosque

tall tower

river

city gate

city wall

archaeologists

ancient site

ruins

Architect's notebook
Town planning

large temples

pyramids

huge stairways

sports arenas

8

This ancient site at Chichen Itza in Mexico was built more than 1,400 years ago, and the architects designed it especially for the needs of the people. They created a well-organized town. Even though it is ancient, it is still a very good example of the sort of town planning we use today.

Pyramids and ball courts in Chichen Itza

his plan shows housing, market places, pyramid temples, public aths, water sources, and ball courts or sports built close to each other. he streets crisscross the area to nk it all together so that every part f the **community** is easy to reach.

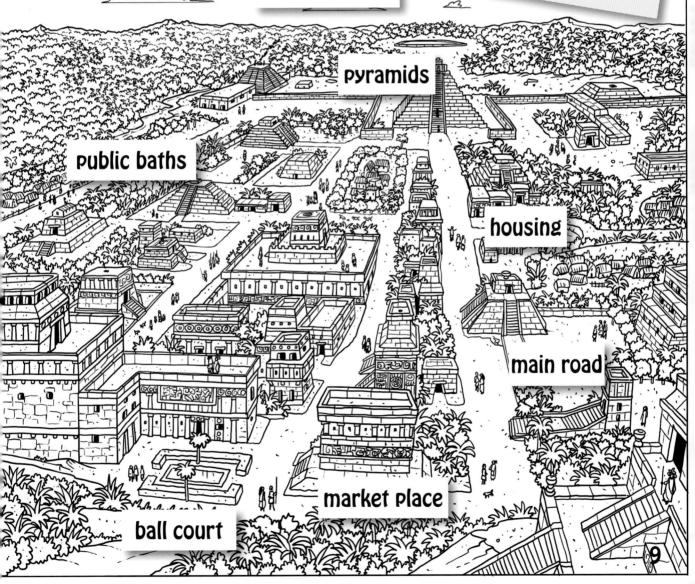

water source

pyramids

public baths

housing

main road

market place

ball court

9

Museums

It's good to know how people used to live, but books and pictures can't tell the whole story. Today, there are special open-air museums which are designed to bring ancient villages back to life.

The Bukchon Hanok Village near Seoul, South Korea, recreates the smells, sights, and sounds of long ago. It includes traditional homes such as this Hanok that has a **thatched** roof and porch area. The house looks just like it did 600 years ago!

Sometimes, these living museums have people dressed in traditional clothing that act out scenes to show how people lived in olden times. The actors might invite visitors to take part in a typical day at work or school. They might teach how to make certain crafts or food from long ago, which can also be cooked and tasted.

An old-fashioned school room with wooden desks in the Skansen Museum, Sweden

A traditional Batak home

The Huta Bolon museum in Sumatra, Indonesia, also shows traditional music and dance.

The museum has some Batak homes, too. They were shared by several families and their animals! The **structure** was built on wooden posts, with a ladder up to the front door, and the sweeping roof was beautifully carved and painted.

11

Choosing a site

In ancient times, deciding where to build a home was very important. Often there was a special reason to choose a particular site.

Machu Picchu is a city located high in the Andes Mountains in Peru. It was built over 500 years ago and ever since it was discovered, archaeologists have been studying it to discover more about the Inca tribe who lived there.

A view of Machu Picchu

People believe that Machu Picchu was built for the Emperor Pachacuti as a place for him to relax and take a break from ruling his **empire**. Still, it was also a working city, and there were several reasons to choose this particular place to build:

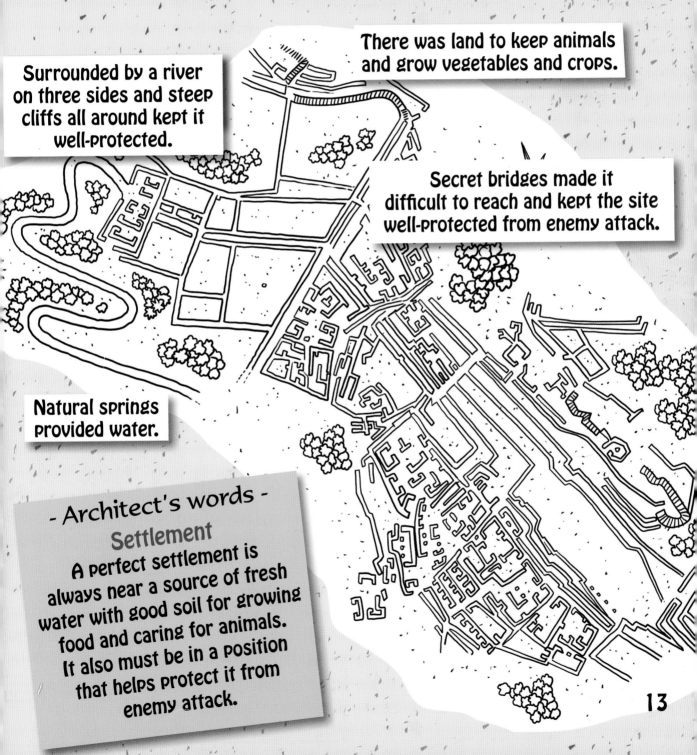

There was land to keep animals and grow vegetables and crops.

Surrounded by a river on three sides and steep cliffs all around kept it well-protected.

Secret bridges made it difficult to reach and kept the site well-protected from enemy attack.

Natural springs provided water.

- Architect's words -
Settlement
A perfect settlement is always near a source of fresh water with good soil for growing food and caring for animals. It also must be in a position that helps protect it from enemy attack.

13

What do we need?

When choosing a site for a settlement, a few important things must be considered.

soil
Is the soil rich with nutrients and good for growing crops? Is there food for the animals to graze on?

water
Is the site near a source of fresh water, such as a river, lake, spring, or sink hole? Water is essential because nothing can live without it.

natural supplies
What other things can be used that are found in the area naturally? It could include trees for building or even gold or diamonds for mining.

defense

A good site offers safety from enemies or wild animals. It may be high up, with a good view of everything below. It might be a place that is difficult to reach or has a secret entrance.

building materials

Building a settlement is easier when the materials needed can be found near the site. Things such as stone, clay, or wood are useful.

climate

The type of **climate** and **weather** in the area are important. Harsh climates with extremely hot summers or very cold winters can cause problems.

15

Architect's notebook
Ancient tools

Just like today, ancient architects were excellent at math. They had to be because they needed to know the exact measurements of all their designs. It was important to make sure that all the buildings were safe and strong.

Tools and technology also provided help when designing buildings. Along with a pen and piece of paper, they would have also used a ruler, a square, and two different types of compass.

A compass was used for finding north, south, east, and west, but also more specific directions.

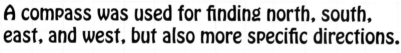

A wooden ruler with a metal bar, called a square, was used to draw right angles.

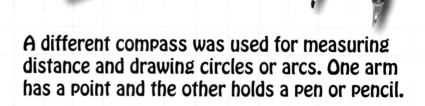

A different compass was used for measuring distance and drawing circles or arcs. One arm has a point and the other holds a pen or pencil.

Ancient technology

When it came to building, an ancient **construction team** didn't have machinery like we do today—no cranes, bulldozers, diggers, or electric drills. They had to do it all by hand.

However, they were very creative and developed technology that allowed them to do high quality work. For example, in Ancient Egypt, they moved enormous stones without machinery. They either dragged the heavy stones on sleds over the wet sand or they used ropes to pull them over top of logs, which acted like wheels.

17

Architect's notebook
Air flow chimneys

Termite mounds have a special design that controls the temperature inside their home! This idea is so smart that architects have used it in their own plans for buildings around the world.

Termites hate to be hot! One species called the compass termite builds a tall, thin mound so the mound never gets too much sun on its surface.

Termites also use air conditioning. They create a chimney through the center of the mound and make lots of holes all over the structure.

Then, by opening and closing the holes during the day, they are able to let warm air out of the top and bring cool air in at the base.

warm air

cool air

Termite mounds can be as high as ten feet (three meters)!

Catalhöyük

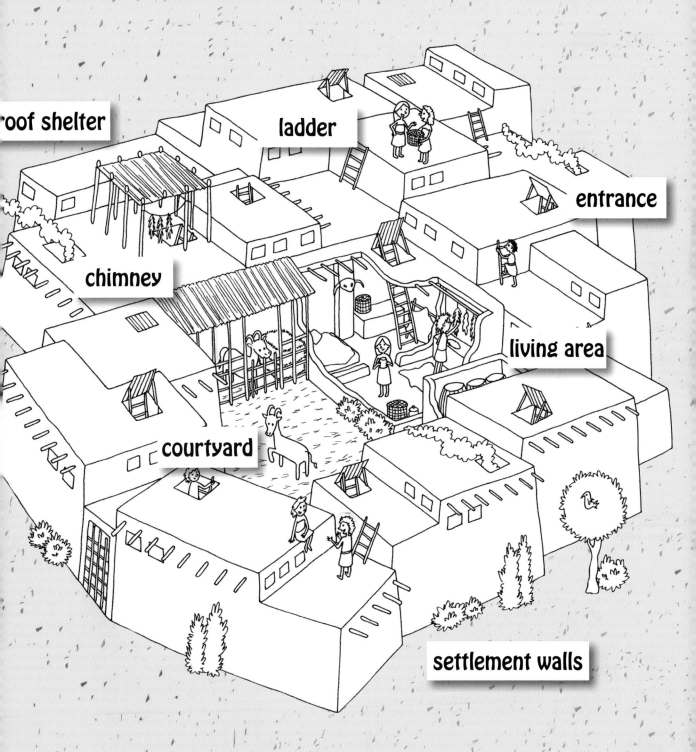

roof shelter

ladder

entrance

chimney

living area

courtyard

settlement walls

Petra

Petra is a beautiful city in Jordan. It is also called Rose City because the buildings are carved out of the pink rock found there. It is one of the world's most famous archaeological sites.

Some of the structures are over 2,000 years old, but they are still standing strong. The structures show the detailed architecture from that time. Designs include tall columns, carefully carved roof decorations, and grand porches.

The buildings are partly carved into the rock and partly built against it.

Petra has the best protection from its enemies because it is hidden behind rocks as tall as skyscrapers. The only way in is through a narrow passage.

20

Architect's notebook
Water engineering

Even though Petra is in the desert, it always had water from a nearby stream. Still, that was not enough to survive all year round because there were often droughts, or long periods of no rain. So the people who created this city also designed technology to store and channel any water.

The engineers in Petra designed strong **dams** to stop water from flowing away. They used special systems called **cisterns** and **reservoirs** for storing the water. Long channels transported the water around the city.

One of the water channels in Petra

Aqueducts are another well-designed form of ancient water channel. They are like long bridges with tall columns built to carry water across wide valleys.

In ancient times, most people didn't have a bathroom in their home. They visited public places to bathe or go to the toilet!

Ancient toilets

Public baths in Bath, England

23

Flooded!
The story of Atlantis

For thousands of years, people have told the story of a beautiful land named Atlantis. It is said to have been a group of islands, each ruled by one of the ten sons of Poseidon, the Greek god of the sea.

It was a very rich country containing magnificent buildings with silver and gold walls. The roofs were made of other valuable materials such as copper and precious ivory from elephant tusks.

The people of Atlantis were very happy. They grew fruit to eat and bathed in hot springs. The kingdom became strong and powerful.

However, something terrible happened. No one knows if it was an enormous earthquake or an eruption from a volcano...

...but the island of Atlantis was suddenly completely destroyed. It sank and disappeared forever under the sea!

Many people think this is just a fairytale or myth, but others believe it is real and are still searching for this lost empire.

Pompeii

About 2,000 years ago, a volcano in Italy known as Mount Vesuvius erupted and completely covered the nearby town of Pompeii in ash and stone.

It happened so quickly that everything was trapped on the spot, as if it had been frozen in time. Years later, archaeologists cleared away the top layers of ash and discovered this ancient **Roman** city looked the same as it had thousands of years before.

Most people lived in quite simple homes with just a few rooms and usually in a building shared with other families.

The city of Pompeii as it looks today

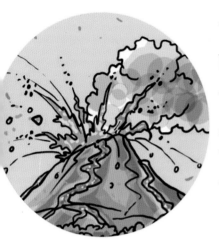

The homes of the rich were large buildings with entrance halls, storage rooms, living and dining areas, and big gardens. These houses were centrally heated with hot air and had toilets, bathrooms, and running water.

The architects of Pompeii built strong houses, temples, theaters, and stores. They constructed roads for travel and public baths where people would bathe and meet friends.

- Archaeologist's words -
Excavation
When an archaeologist thinks an ancient site is buried underground, a team of people carefully dig down through the top layers of soil and rock to find what is underneath. This is called an excavation.

New or old technology?

Today, the ancient Romans are remembered all over the world for their architecture, engineering, and technology.

Roman designs have lasted for centuries. They have given us a lot of ideas for modern technology. These ideas include the way we heat our homes...

Underfloor heating—Roman (above) and modern (below)

- Architect's notes -
Underfloor heating
This is a special type of central heat that uses pipes underneath the floor that are filled with a liquid such as water. When the water warms up, the floor gets warm, too. The heat then rises into the air and increases the temperature of the room.

...to how we build our roads...

Modern road building

Roman road

...and how we decorate our homes and surroundings.

Roman mosaic

A modern mosaic in Barcelona, Spain

ACTIVITY: DESIGN YOUR OWN MOSAIC

A mosaic is a picture made of little tiles. The people of Pompeii built mosaics into the walls and floors of their homes. Here's how you can make one yourself...

1. Cut some different colored sheets of paper into small squares.
2. On a big piece of paper, draw a large outline of your picture or design.
3. Glue the colored paper squares onto the outline to create lines, shades, and patterns.

Glossary

aqueduct A channel used to carry water long distances or across valleys

archaeologist A scientist who studies ancient sites to learn about the people and ways of the past

cistern A storage tank for water

climate The average or typical weather over a long period of time in a region

community A group of people living close together

construction team A group of people who who work together to build a structure

dam A structure in a river designed and built to stop the flow of water

empire A group of countries ruled by an emperor or empress

engineering Using math, science, and creative thinking to design many of the things in our world

fortified Something that is strong and secure

materials The objects used to construct a home

reservoir A large lake, either natural or human-made, used as a water supply

Roman A word to describe the people and things of ancient Rome and its empire

site A place or location where a building will be placed.

structure Another name for the framework of a building

thatch A type of roof covering using straw or leaves

weather The outside conditions of air and temperature at a certain time and place

Learning more

Books:

Halstead, Rachel. *Hand-On History Projects: Home Life.* London: Anness, 2009.
The projects in this book help readers learn about ancient homes and life in different regions of the world.

Harrison, Paul. *Ancient Roman Homes.* New York: Powerkids Press, 2010.
Learn about the homes of both the rich and the poor and discover what the lives of the people that lived in them was like.

Horning, Johathan. *Simple Shelters: Tents, Tipis, Yurts, Domes and Other Ancient Homes.* London: Walker & Company, 2009.
This book brings an introduction to the history of shelters and their construction.

Websites:

http://www.ancientgreece.co.uk/dailylife/challenge/cha_set.html
Learn about the homes of the Ancient Greek by playing the House Challenge Game.

www.mummies2pyramids.info/daily-life/egyptian-house.htm
Read and look at pictures about life and homes in ancient Egypt.

www.ducksters.com/history/ancient_rome/pompeii.php
Learn more about the city of Pompeii and the day it got buried under a thick layer of ash. Afterward, take a short quiz to test what you have learned.

Index